VOLUME 7

FOR YOUNGER CHILDREN

Produced and Arranged by Chris Marion

Companion Products:

Cassette Leader's Guide 0-6330-1620-9
(Contains teaching materials, video, listening cassette, split-track
accompaniment cassette, and printed piano accompaniments)

CD Leader's Guide 0-6330-1621-7
(Contains teaching materials, video, listening CD, split-track
accompaniment CD, and printed piano accompaniments)

Listening Cassette 0-6330-1618-7
(available at a reduced price when bought in quantities of 10 or more)

Listening CD 0-6330-1619-5
(available at a reduced price when bought in quantities of 10 or more)

Printed Piano Accompaniments 0-6330-1617-9

Cassette Promo Pak 0-6330-1622-5

CD Promo Pak 0-6330-1623-3

0-6330-1616-0

Producer and Arranger
Chris Marion

Track Sequencer
Chris Marion

Piano Transcriptions and Music Engraving
Compute-A-Chart, Allen Tuten

Video Production
Summit Video Production
Oklahoma City, OK
Anita Wagoner, Producer

Layout and Art Supervisor
Unlikely Suburban Design

Illustrator
Dan Brawner

Cover Art
Maksimowicz Design

Teaching and Worship Plans
Pam Andrews, Nan Grantham, and Pamela Vandewalker

Project Coordinator
Alyssa Goins

CONTENTS

It's Always the Right Time

Words and Music by
JANET McMAHAN-WILSON and TOM McBRYDE
Arranged by Chris Marion

Everybody Sing Praise

Words and Music by
JOHN CHISUM and NANCY GORDON
Arranged by Chris Marion

Praise Him

Words and Music by
DENNIS JERNIGAN
Arranged by Chris Marion

22

Praise, _____

Je - sus, _ my Mas - ter, _ took me from . dis - as - ter and

Sin is _ de - feat - ed _ and now He _ is seat - ed, the

24

praise _____ Him. |1, 2, 3 _ Him. |4

He is _ the rea - son _ I sing.

King is _ en - throned on _ my praise.   praise.

BOTH PARTS
mp

27

Praise _____ Him,   praise _____ Him.

31

Praise, _____   praise _____ Him.

mf

35

Praise _____ Him,   praise _____ Him.

39

Praise, _____   praise _____ Him.

43

Praise _____ Him,   praise _____ Him.

I've Got the Love of Jesus

Words and Music by
JOHN CHISUM and NANCY GORDON
Arranged by Chris Marion

The Great Commission

Words and Music by
JIMMY TRAVIS GETZEN
Arranged by Chris Marion

I Gotta Tell Somebody

Words and Music by
LINDA L. WALKER
Arranged by Chris Marion

I Am the Light

Words and Music by
PAMELA CLAMPITT VANDEWALKER
and RHONDA BARNETT
Arranged by Chris Marion

I am the Light, the Light of the world, he that fol-lows Me shall nev-er walk in dark-ness. Oh, ___

I am the Light, the Light of the world, he that fol-lows Me shall have the Light of life.

First time - SOLO 1
Second time - SOLO 2

1. Dark-ness can be scat-tered ___ with the light of love. It
2. On-ly takes one light ___ to bright-en up a room. And

is a spe-cial gift that comes from God a-bove.
I will be that light 'cause He is com-ing soon.

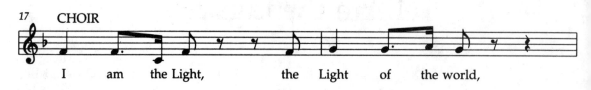

17 CHOIR

I am the Light, the Light of the world,

19

He that fol-lows Me shall nev - er walk in dark-ness. Oh, ___

21

I am the Light, the Light of the world,

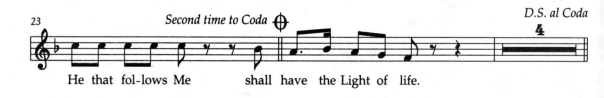

23 *Second time to Coda* $\oplus$ *D.S. al Coda*

4

He that fol-lows Me shall have the Light of life.

29 $\oplus$ CODA

have the Light of life. He that fol - lows Me shall

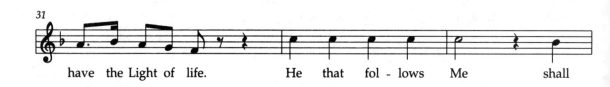

31

have the Light of life. He that fol - lows Me shall

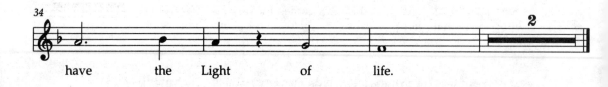

34

2

have the Light of life.

Tell the Good News

Words and Music by
GENE BARLETT
Arranged by Chris Marion

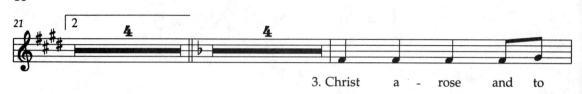

21

3. Christ a - rose and to

30

heav - en went, __ Tell the good news, __

32

tell the good news; __ All may fol - low __ who re - pent, __

35

Tell the good news, __ tell the good news. __

37

Tell the good news, __ tell the good news, __

39

Tell the good news __ that Christ has come; Tell the good news, __

42

tell the good news; __ Tell the good news __ to ev - 'ry - one.

45

Tell the good news __ to ev - 'ry - one.

EVERY GOOD THING

Stepping

Skipping

17

OH, WHAT A DAY!

Be sharp ♯ This is a sharp ♯
A sharp raises a pitch ½ step.

Find the sharps of the following notes
on the keyboard provided.

C-C♯   D-D♯   F-F♯   G-G♯   A-A♯

C♯   D♯   F♯   G♯   A♯

C D E F G A B

RHYTHM IN A BOX

Count: ‖: ♩   ♩   ♩   ♩ :‖
     1   2   3   4

Count: ‖: ♫   ♫   ♫   ♫ :‖
    1 & 2 & 3 & 4 &

Count: ‖: ♫   ♫   ♫   ♫ :‖
    1 & 2 & 3 & 4 &

OBEDIACT!

The greatest way to show our love for Jesus is to be obedient.

CHANT PRAISE!

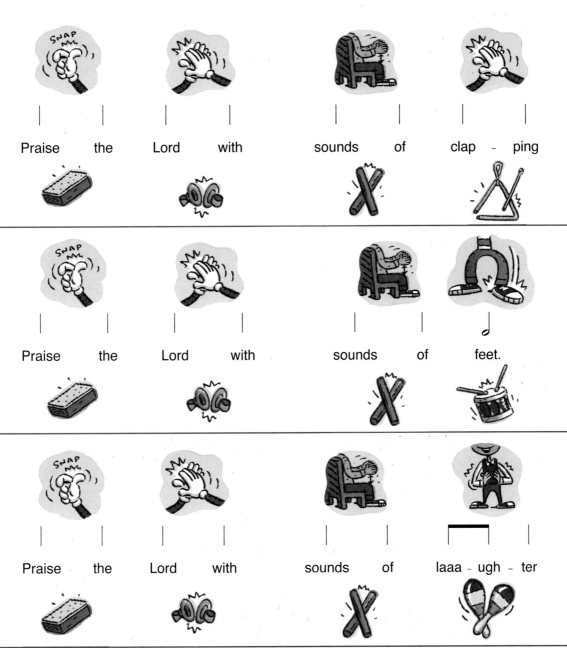

Praise the Lord with sounds of clap - ping

Praise the Lord with sounds of feet.

Praise the Lord with sounds of laaa - ugh - ter

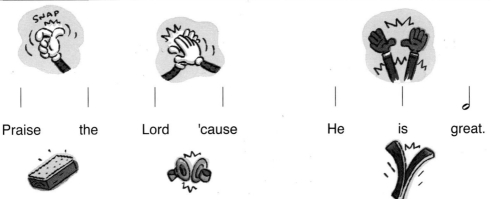

Praise the Lord 'cause He is great.

RIGHT TIME REBUS

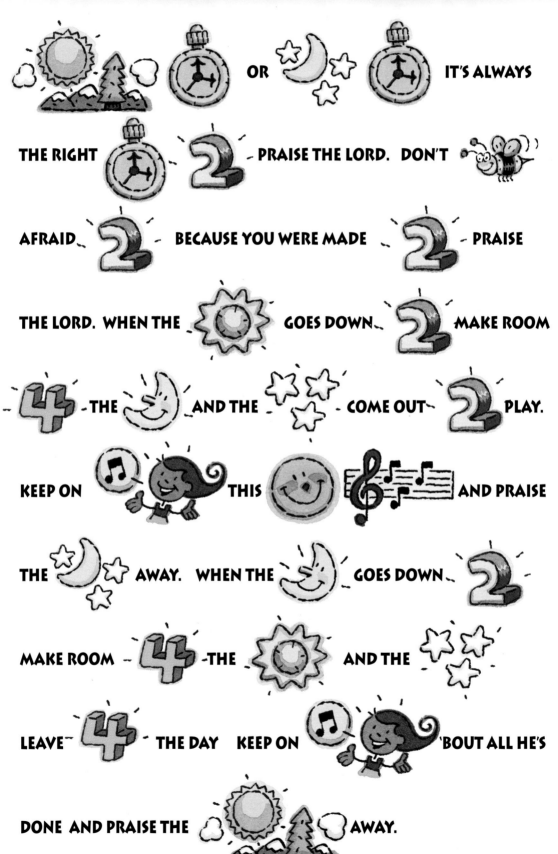

SUN OVER MOUNTAINS [DAY] TIME OR NIGHT TIME IT'S ALWAYS THE RIGHT TIME 2 PRAISE THE LORD. DON'T BEE AFRAID 2 BECAUSE YOU WERE MADE 2 PRAISE THE LORD. WHEN THE SUN GOES DOWN 2 MAKE ROOM 4 THE MOON AND THE STARS COME OUT 2 PLAY. KEEP ON SINGING THIS SONG AND PRAISE THE MOON STARS AWAY. WHEN THE MOON GOES DOWN 2 MAKE ROOM 4 THE SUN AND THE STARS LEAVE 4 THE DAY KEEP ON SINGING 'BOUT ALL HE'S DONE AND PRAISE THE SUN AWAY.

22

THE HAND OF SALVATION

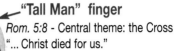

"Tall Man" finger
Rom. 5:8 - Central theme: the Cross
"... Christ died for us."

Ring finger
Rom. 10:9-10
Commitment
"If you confess
with your
mouth 'Jesus
is Lord . . .' "

"Pointer" finger
Rom. 3:23
Points to all
"All have
sinned ..."

John 10:10 "...I am come that they may have life, and have it to the full."

Romans 3:23 "For all have sinned and fall short of the glory of God."

Romans 5:8 "But God demonstrates His own love for us in this: While we were still sinners, Christ died for us."

Romans 10:9-10 "That if you confess with your mouth, Jesus is Lord, and believe in your heart that God raised Him from the dead, you will be saved. For it is with your heart that you believe and are justified, and it is with your mouth that you confess and are saved."

Ephesians 2:8-9 "For it is by grace you have been saved, through faith—and this is not from yourselves, it is the gift of God—not by works, so that no one can boast."

"Pinkie" (or little) finger
Eph. 2:8-9
a little
counts! ...
saved
through
faith...the
gift of God.

Thumb
John 10:10
Thumbs up!
Good news ...
that they may
have life, and
have it to the full.

23

LET EVERYTHING PRAISE THE LORD

STEADY BEAT CHART

To find the steady beat in this song, touch each dot on every beat.

LIGHT IN THE NIGHT

"I AM THE LIGHT"
John 8:12

PLATES

A SANDWICH OR A CHORD

We can think of a chord like we think of a sandwich — a filling between 2 pieces of bread.

A ham sandwich tastes like ham because it has ham in the middle. What happens when we change the ham to another kind of filling?

Now the sandwich tastes different. The filling in the middle makes it taste like a cheese sandwich.

A chord is a "note" sandwich—2 notes on top and bottom, with a note in the middle. The middle note can be changed, and the chord will have a different sound.

This chord is a major chord. Some people say it has a happy sound.

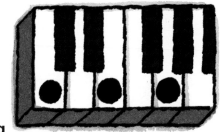

By changing the middle note (moving it just 1 piano note to the left), the sound changes to a sad or mysterious sound. This is a minor chord.

Listen for the mysterious sounds in "Brave Queen Ester."

TELL THE GOOD NEWS!

An angel came to Mary
And said, "Please have no fear,
For you will have a Baby.
God will be with us here."

An angel came to Joseph
"Your Mary is with Child.
And you will call Him Jesus,
So gentle and so mild."

Angels came to shepherds,
With tidings of great joy!
"Go to Bethlehem and see
God's precious Baby Boy!"

Through prophets and through angels
God's promises are heard.
He gives them to us still —
In His Holy Word.

God's Word to us is precious —
A treasure we must share
And tell about our Jesus!
Let's tell it everywhere!

Tell the good news!

Tell the good news!

Tell the good news!

Tell the good news!

THE GIFT OF GOD

Follow the ribbons with your finger to sing connected phrases.

THE FIRST THANKSGIVING

The first Thanks - giv - ing, The

first Thanks - giv - ing on the

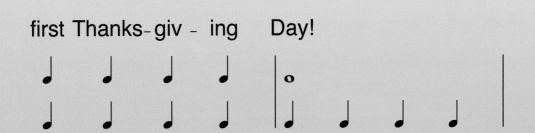

first Thanks - giv - ing Day!

OH, WHO CAN MAKE A
RAINBOW?

First I tried my crayons, and choose them carefully,
But the rainbow on the paper was not like those we see.

Next I got my water paints. I thought they'd mix just fine,
But my paper got all bumpy, and the paint ran off the lines.

Someone said, "Use chalk." and so I rubbed it here and there.
Then looked and I discovered there were smudges everywhere.

I tore bits of paper and glued them on so tight,
But even then, the colors didn't seem to look quite right.

I cut colored streamers and waved them in the air,
But the streamers got all twisted as they swirled around up there.

I even tried balloons—and let them float up high.
They just looked like pretty balls—not a rainbow in the sky.

I learned a little song when I was very small
I know it's words are true now—and a lesson for us all—

"Oh, who can make a rainbow? I'm sure I can't. Can you?
Oh, who can make a rainbow? No one but God is true."

I'm Learning Lessons

Words and Music by
ANITA WAGONER
Arranged by Chris Marion

Brave Queen Esther

Words and Music by
KIRK DEARMAN and NANCY GORDON
Arranged by Chris Marion

Never Again, Noah

Words and Music by
ANITA WAGONER
Arranged by Chris Marion

Let Everything Praise the Lord

Words and Music by
CHRIS and DIANE MACHEN
Arranged by Chris Marion

The Gift of God

Words and Music by
CATHY SPURR and DEBBIE McNEIL
Arranged by Chris Marion

Every Good Thing

Words and Music by
DOUG GRISAFFE and KEITH ANDERSON
Arranged by Chris Marion

ev - 'ry per - fect gift ___ comes

from a - bove. ___ ___

___ from God. ___ Ev-'ry good thing, ev - 'ry good thing,

ev - 'ry good thing comes down ___ from the Fa - ther.

Ev - 'ry good thing, ev - 'ry good thing,

ev - 'ry good thing comes down ___ from God. ___

ev - 'ry good thing comes down ___ from God. ___

Ev - 'ry good thing comes down ___ from God. ___

Isn't He

Words and Music by
RUTH ELAINE SCHRAM
Arranged by Chris Marion

Sav - ior we love. __ Is - n't He the Sav - ior we love? __

Sav - ior we love! __ Look - ing

down from a - bove. __ Is - n't He the Sav - ior we love? __

Sav - ior we love! And ev - 'ry day I'm gon - na

pray, and when I praise Him I will say: He's the

Sav - ior we love. _ Is - n't He the Sav - ior we love? __

He's a won - der - ful Lord, _ He's a

pow - er - ful God, _ He's the Sav - ior we love. _

Is - n't He the Sav - ior we love? __

I Will Trust You

Words and Music by
PAM NOEL
Arranged by Chris Marion

Obedience Is

Words and Music by
JIMMY TRAVIS GETZEN
Arranged by Chris Marion

Oh, What a Day!

Words and Music by
TOM McBRYDE and LYNN S. WILBANKS
Arranged by Chris Marion

Oh, what a day! Oh, what a day! This is the

one. Oh, what a day! Oh, what a day!

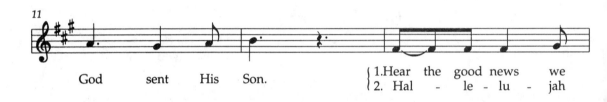

God sent His Son.

1.Hear the good news we
2. Hal - le - lu - jah

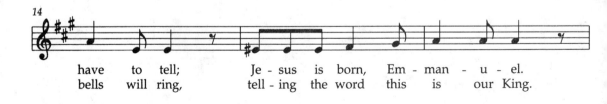

have to tell; Je - sus is born, Em - man - u - el.
bells will ring, tell - ing the word this is our King.

Oh, what a day! Oh, what a day! It's Christ - mas

Day. Day!

Oh, what a day! Oh, what a day! This is the

one. Oh, what a day! Oh, what a day!

God send His Son. Joy to the world, we

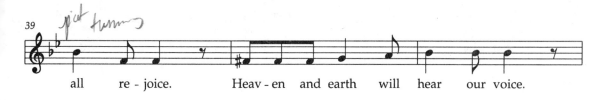

all re - joice. Heav - en and earth will hear our voice.

Oh, what a day! Oh, what a day! It's Christ - mas

Day! Oh, what a day! Oh, what a day!

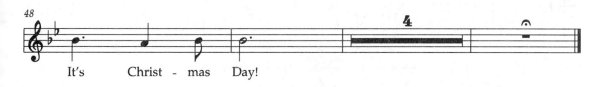

It's Christ - mas Day!

The First Thanksgiving

Words and Music by
LINDA L. WALKER
Arranged by Chris Marion

22
share their food. They all came to-geth-er to give thanks, too. The
25
first Thanks-giv-ing, the first Thanks-giv-ing, on the first Thanks-giv - ing
28
Day! And now we gath - er a -
31
cross the land, with hum - ble hearts we join our hands, we
34
bow our heads to give thanks and pray, and re -
36
mem - ber the first Thanks - giv - ing Day. The
38
first Thanks-giv-ing, the first Thanks-giv-ing, on the first Thanks-giv - ing
41
Day. The first Thanks-giv-ing, the first Thanks-giv-ing, on the
44
first Thanks - giv - ing Day.

He Is Risen

Words and Music by
LINDA L. WALKER
Arranged by Chris Marion